I0171133

Joyful Messages

A relaxing coloring book

for grown-ups

By Caryn Colgan

Express your creative spirit with affirmations and personal art.

Also enjoy her first coloring book called

Color for Health.

ISBN: 978-0-9679616-0-6

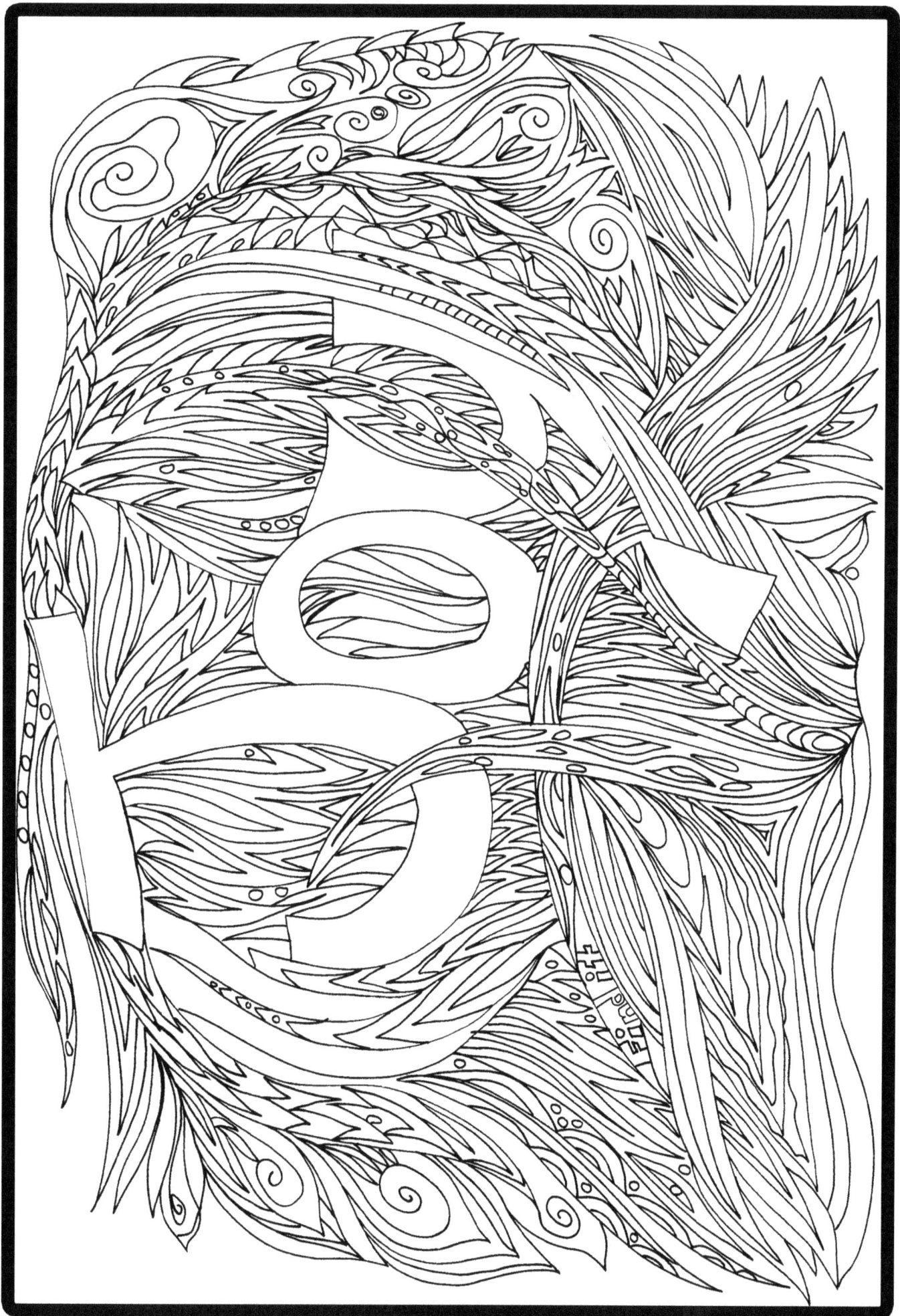

I am respected

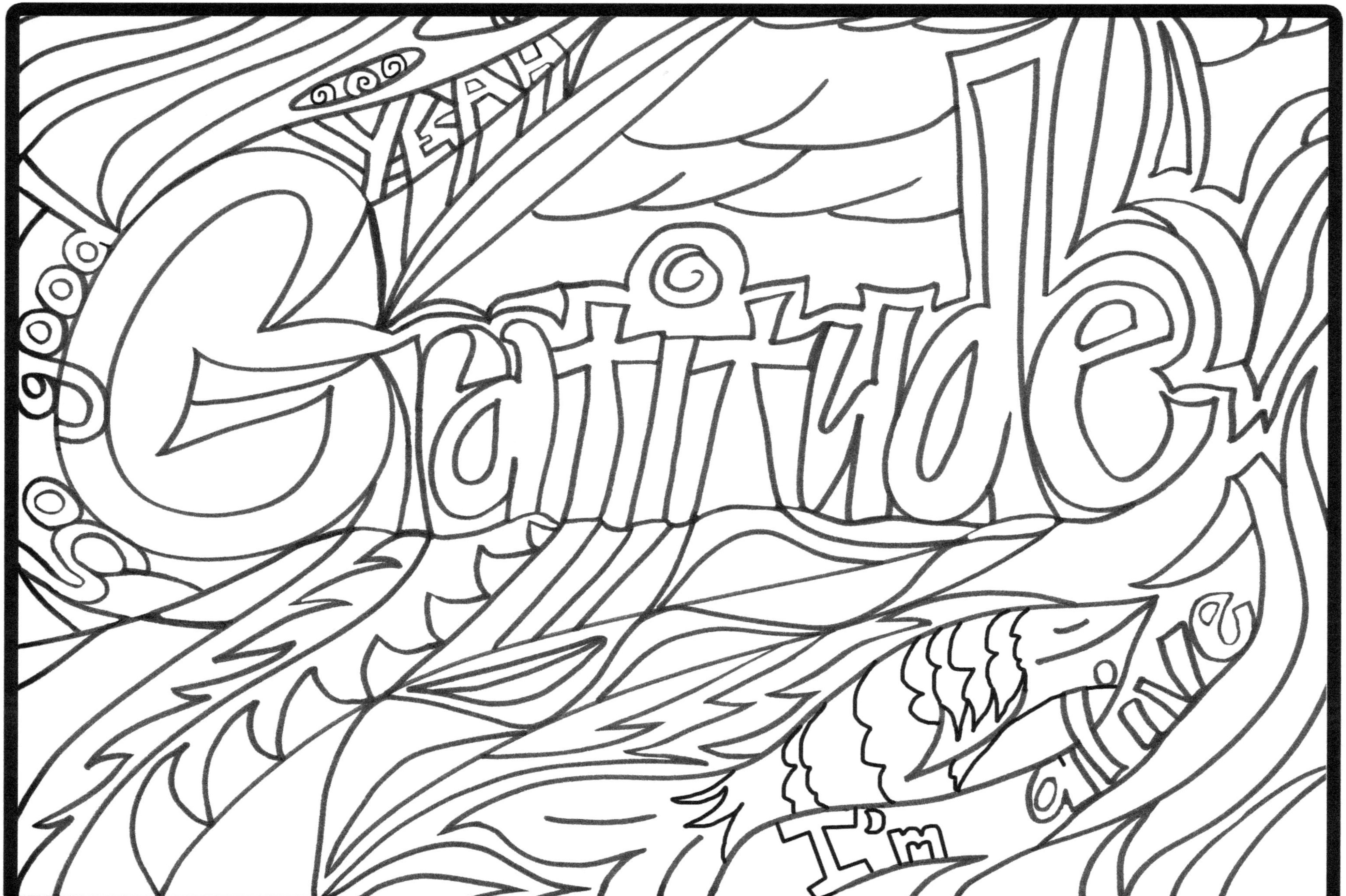

good
YEAH
Gratitude
I'm alive

I Choose Positive Thoughs

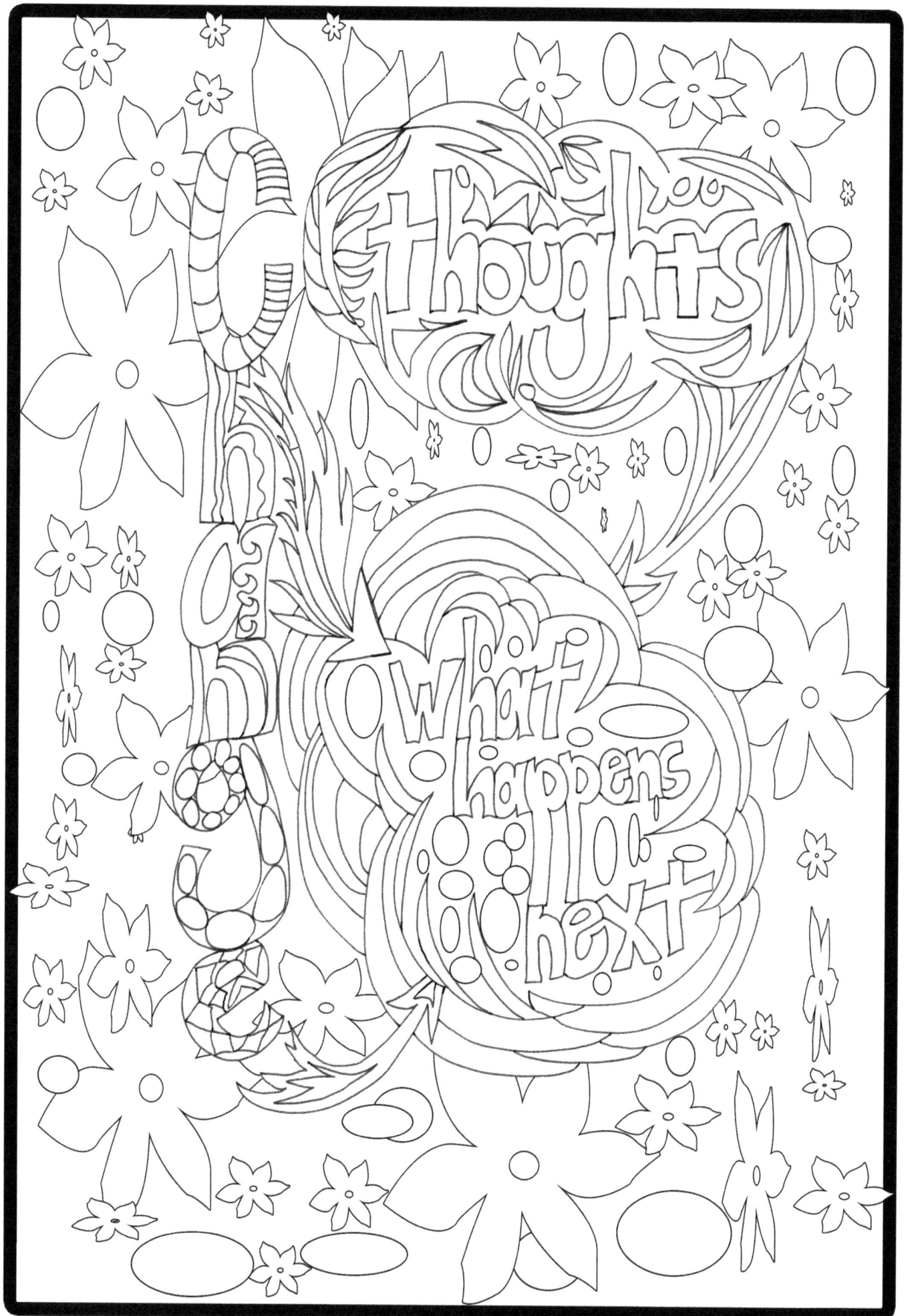

thoughts

what happens next

Answers come

Meditate

Pray

Chant

Listen in Silence

infinite choices

From a sea of

HAPPY ME.

HEAL

Choose

Go fish for it! abundance

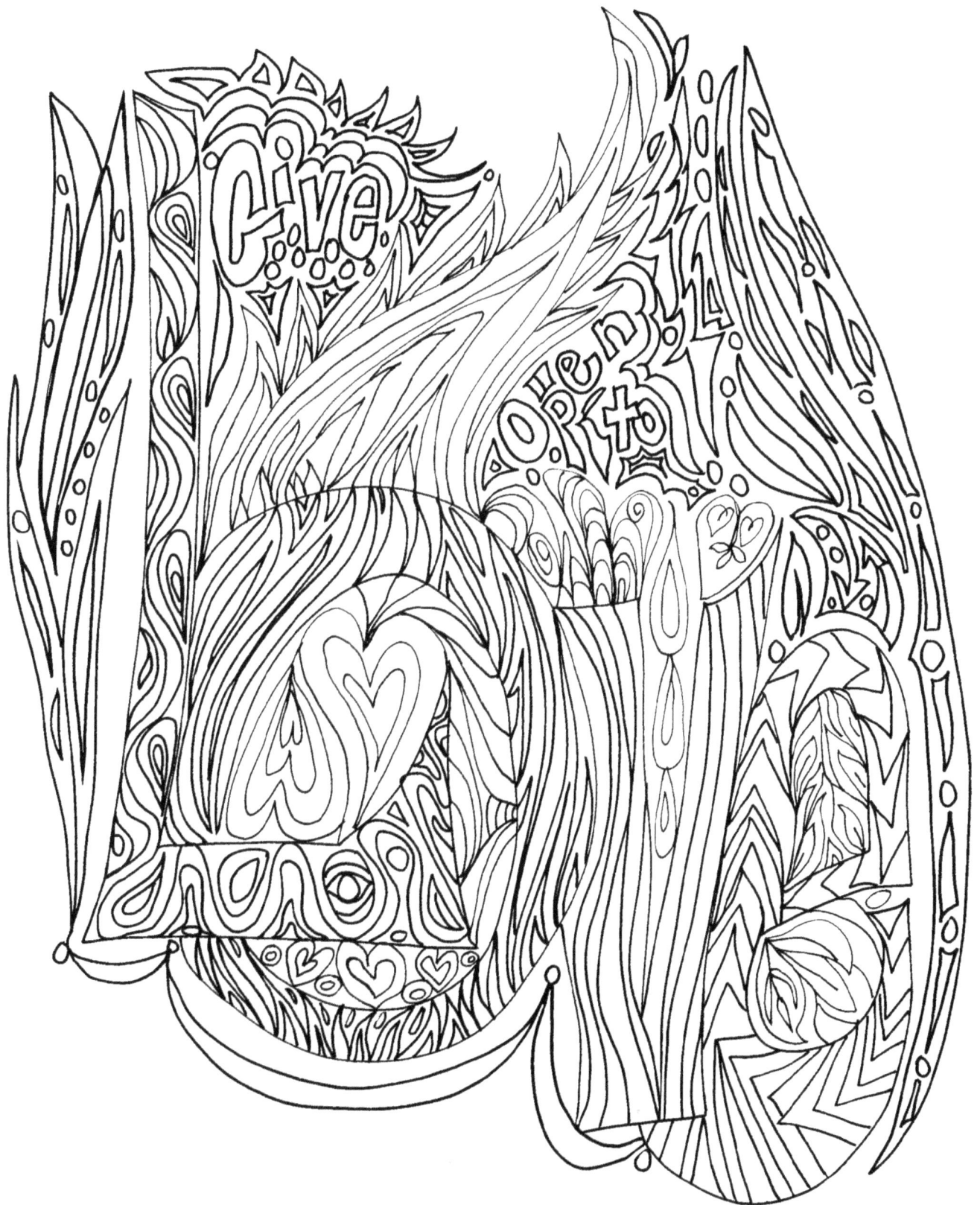

Live

Open to

OPEN TO HEAL

Laugh

Love

Play

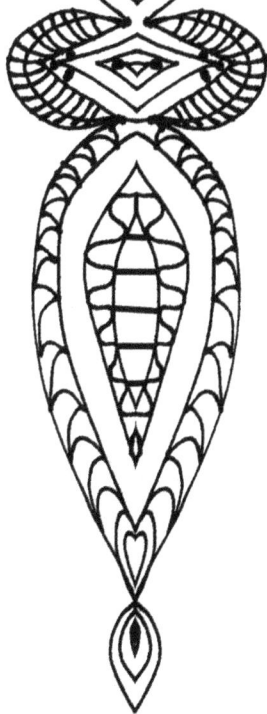

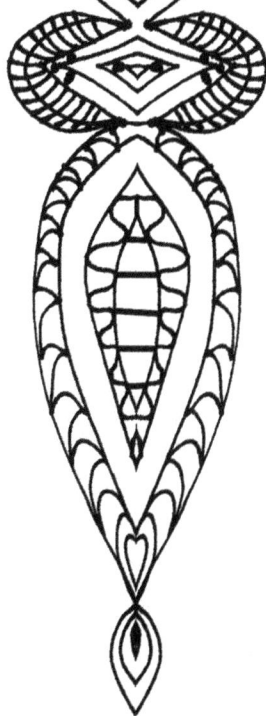

I'm happiest when I smile love guffaw when laugh giggle play scream

www.ingramcontent.com/pod-product-compliance
Lightning Source LLC
Chambersburg PA
CBHW080524030426
42337CB00023B/4627